Black British]

CW00382471

By

MARCELINE POWELL

'An un-layering of the issues behind knife crime, youth

violence and bl**ack boys**'

© 2019 published by Powell and Barns Limited

The increase in youth violence in the UK related to knife crime and so -called gang activity, is the subject of much debate in 2019.

This short book is a personal exploration of the underlying factors. Using empirical research and information on the 'Gang Matrix' the book examines the failure of government and authorities to understand and tackle the causes instead of the symptoms as they relate to young boys in the black community.

I'll start by stating the obvious, which is, knife crime, youth violence, gang activity and the associated issues are in no way exclusive to the Black community in the UK. That said, these issues do appear to disproportionately affect Black families, and this coincides with the disproportionate number of Black people affected by stop and search, the disproportionality of arrests, subsequent prison sentences, lack of male role models and the impact of poverty.

The mainstream media currently carries heart-breaking stories relating to violent crime, gang activity and related deaths almost daily. But outrage only appears to come from the same media, when the victim is not black! The black victim is scrutinised and investigated for their involvement in gangs as though somehow trying to find justifications for senseless murder.

The victims seem to be getting younger, but sympathy for the families and the outrage for the young life lost does not appear when the victim is black.

Families and communities most affected by gang and knife crime are treated like the underclass, the children trapped in these often economically disadvantaged communities are not afforded the sympathy they deserve.

The children caught in the horrific cycle of crime, violence, gangs, drug dealing, and death are not treated as children. Instead they are presented in the media as 'the other' they are 'feared' by wider society and their chances and opportunities are minimal as a result of negative stereotyping.

As a result, it appears that the people who are grooming young children into gangs, those manipulating, threatening and kidnapping children to force them to carry out their dirty work, are getting away with murder. Sometimes literally!

Let us address some of the glaring issues that we do not see all over the mainstream media but do exist in the real world, in communities where people are in fear for their children's lives. Literally!

Many people can be forgiven for accepting the media portrayal of knife crime perpetrators being 'unruly' young people with no 'family structure' or 'lack of male role models'. This is the picture that is so often painted after all. The problem with this portrayal is that it provides a comfortable 'othering process' that can entice some families into a false sense of security where they believe that this issue cannot affect them because they do not fit the stereotype. The bad news is, these stereotypes are a myth and the threat of knife crime is not exclusive to a 'type' of family. Any young person with friends, a social life and exposed to peer pressure - or worse - a drug habit or bullying, can be exposed to this issue.

The bias media portrayal is also responsible for misinforming us about the deeper and more disturbing dynamics of violent gangs and as such misses talking about the extremely high number of young people who are involved under duress.

The UK currently has a big issue with people inside prison wielding power on the streets. These criminals are usually older, and usually they are seasoned criminals, they are well known on the 'streets' with a history of violence and a history of serving time in prison. They know the system well and they do not fear it.

Even from inside the prison system they are 'giving orders' to younger boys on the outside and these 'orders can include a range of things from dealing drugs to carrying out an attack on a rival. The younger person who receives the order is not given a choice, it is simply a case of do as they are told, if they do not follow orders, they risk becoming the victim of a violent attack themselves.

In some parts of the country we hear reports within the community of sexual grooming, whereby a 'younger' / youth will be forced to carry out some sort of sexual act as an initiation into a 'gang'. This ensures the abuser has power over the abused and guarantees the loyalty and silence of the abuse victim through shame and embarrassment.

3

Further still, there are those young men who have found economic success through music, despite being involved in drug dealing or violent crime, they have received enough air play on mainstream media to become celebrities. The music they are producing encourages territorial violence, it discourages resolution and yet they are being promoted on mainstream stations. Worst still, some of these 'so called' music 'artists' are rumoured to be using their new-found economic status to control younger boys and support them into drug dealing and providing the young gangs with knives for use as weapons.

I approach this topic with questions. Why aren't communities, and the authorities treating the gangs who groom young people into gang activity in a similar way to any other groomer? Why is there such reluctance to have an honest and open discussion about what is going on behind the scenes with many so called 'gangs.

Why is it that local groups who work with children and young people are struggling to find resources when so many young people are dying as a result of senseless violence. Furthermore, when we do see a community group featured in the media, they're rarely working with the young people who are directly involved.

Of course, all young people should be able to access the support they need however, conversations and statistics are futile if we then ignore the recurring factors and trends such as the disproportionate number of Black and ethnic minority families becoming victims of 'gang' related or drug related knife crime and violence, or the higher ranking drug dealers who are making big money from addiction and death whilst young vulnerable people are stopped, searched, arrested and sentenced - quickly replaced in the gang by another young person.

What is being done about the people in prison controlling younger boys and operating as invisible ring leaders?

Why aren't we seeing or discussing the child protection issues that are so glaringly obvious?

If an older person, an adult, by definition, is enticing a young impressionable child into activities that will lead them to harm. If an adult is putting a child under duress, or threat to carry out or participate in activities that are harmful (mentally, emotionally or physically) this is a safeguarding issue, a mental health issue, a child protection issue.

The glamour would soon be removed, and the seriousness of this situation would be reinforced if the children in these cases were being treated as children who are vulnerable, exposed to graphic, disturbing, life changing incidents that lead to fear and PTSD.

4

Children are being criminalised instead of being treated as victims

Recently the Met police filmed and broadcast a raid on a house as part of a 'county lines' investigation and publicised the fact that among the 'gang' they found a 14-year-old boy who, along with the adults in the 'gang' was also arrested. This should cause concern, using young children is an example of a disturbing layer to the 'gang' and violent crime epidemic that we are watching spiral out of control.

The children are not being treated as 'victim' instead they are being criminalised, when they have potentially and most probably experienced trauma that will no doubt continue to affect them for years to come. Their lives have certainly been changed by the things they have been exposed to. Yet these children are treated the same or similar, to the criminal that has groomed them, or forced them into situations they do not want to be in.

Whoever you are, whatever your colour, culture, profession or parental status. Just ask yourself how you would feel if you found out that a child you love has been befriended, or bullied, or threatened into carrying out acts such as stabbing someone for fear of being stabbed themselves if they do not carry out the 'job'?

How would you feel if you found out a child you love, has been scared for their safety or their lives every time they left the house but were too scared to confide in anyone?

Imagine if they were taken away to a city or town that they did not know and forced to sell drugs or hurt other people as a condition of being able to return home?

Imagine a child you know and love, being forced under threat of violence to carry out sexual acts as part of a gang. Combine, the fear with the humiliation and the feeling of isolation and loneliness and decide for yourself if these scenarios do not have a damaging mental and emotional effect on a young child or teenager.

We know from other examples where children are groomed, that the parents and families of the young victim, are usually the last to know that their children have been at risk.

Part of the process of the groomer, is often to befriend the victim and gain trust or the other extreme is to create fear so that the child feels unable to confide in someone they might trust. In other words, the groomer is usually clever at finding ways to prevent the child from speaking out about what they are experiencing.

This same process is being used by gangs grooming children on our streets. We are now discovering that sexual abuse is being used for gang initiation and yet the mass population believe that this is a 'choice' being made by children. Especially when the situation involves young Black children.

5

Strategic Solutions Needed to Tackle Gang Grooming & Violent Crime

It is frustrating to witness the ongoing debates about tackling gang grooming and violent crime that is both taking and ruining young lives. Surely it is not rocket science!

Let's look at what the authorities could be doing now, besides scratching their heads and reiterating that they don't know how to tackle this issue effectively. Although I certainly do not claim to have all the answers. I am one of many who has been personally affected by these issues and I am certain that the current approach is wrong, and ignorant on so many levels.

If the government and authorities refuse to acknowledge the social and economic issues affecting many young people who find themselves enticed by the 'gang' culture, every effort to tackle this culture is a waste of time. Stop and search can be effective when it is intelligence led however, this approach and the subsequent prison sentences of those found guilty of a crime only solves part of the problem.

We are living in a society where videos of violent activity are circulated on social media for entertainment and discussion. People have become desensitised to the graphic visual display of violence through many reasons, TV, Video games, Music – but in the world of social media addiction, we watch real life violent scenarios without a flinch. People are making big money from perpetuating violence, but black people are experiencing those levels of fear and death in real life.

Sadly, people appear most desensitised to violence between or inflicted upon black men and women. Examples include; CCTV footage clearly showing a young black man being attacked by a police officer, the young man losing his life and the officer walking free. Or the videos on social media of a young black men being arrested by 5 or 6 officers, they were kneeling in his back and spraying CS gas directly into his face at close range while a crowd of angry black people looked on.

 And that is part of the problem. People have stopped reacting to these scenes, instead they look on and ask, "What did the black boy do"? not "Why is it necessary to manhandle and kill"? Even people from the black community have become 'trained' to stand and watch this type of violence being afflicted on young black men and not intervene.

6

Race, Class and Identity

A big part of the problem goes back to the media, the music, video games and movies, they criminalise us as Black men and women, and some young people are influenced by these stereotypes which form their identity and result in them criminalising themselves.

Whether young black people are aware of it or not, the issue of violent crime and so-called gang activity are all directly and intrinsically linked to the institutional racism and classism that still – albeit quietly - plagues Britain. It is present at every level, from school to work place to celebrity.

Young black people are trained to be 'voiceless' by this society. They see or hear negative stereotypes about their parents, their communities, their prospects for the future.

We cannot underestimate the impact these, and other stereotypes have on young people. If they see every person they respect being treated with disrespect, it is only a matter of time before they are likely to react. They lose respect, they demand a respect they have never had. And before you know it, we see a cycle of frustration and bad decision making like the ones we witness today. Despite being influenced by music celebrities and sports people and the like, we cannot even call on celebrity influencers to appeal to these young people because they too (the celebrities) are treated badly by mainstream media if they try to be a representative voice or speak out.

I refer to sports, or music and entertainment because these are examples of where Black people are celebrated until the moment, they speak out about something important, if they use their influence to improve racial stereotypes or – God forbid – if they support a Black cause or civil rights injustice, they are persecuted by the media. It is like a silent command for them to act like a good 'n' boy. Yet people make millions from exploiting these Black celebrities and stars. It is like they really are required to sell their souls for money, their silence has been paid for.

7

The Un-layering process

All this leads to one main point. Talk is cheap and the efforts so far to tackle or address the issues of violent crime are at best, weak.

Without un-layering and readdressing many levels of social inequality and the Psychological effects of negative stereotyping, poor attainment, limited access to resources and opportunities, the police. Courts and prison system, low self-esteem and many more issues that are affecting young black people before they even reach adulthood, without that, talk is futile and very cheap.

If the government refuses to develop a strategy for young people being released from prison, it almost seems pointless sending them to prison in the first place.

The statistics show that only 17% - a very small number of young people - released from prison find a job in the first year. This is a worrying statistic that cannot be ignored. What is in place to assist young people to secure work and an alternative income and move away from criminal activities? What is in place to deal with the impact prison can often have on a young person's mental health? What is in place to deal with the impact on a young person who has witnessed violence or violent death within their personal circle? The answer seems to be nothing! They are most often left in a cycle of crime - reoffending that leads to more lengthy prison sentences - and exposure to the most hardened criminals.

Equally, if dangerous people are still able to wield power from inside prison, the issues continue regardless of the prison sentence passed to a ring leader. And to take things one step further, without a post sentence strategy, communities are left to deal with the fall out amongst criminals who are released from prison after long sentences and brought back into communities where they face old rivals, leading to more violence.

8

Dedicated contact points and support

The young people in these scenarios should be the priority. They need to be encouraged to speak about their experiences. They should be provided with confidential contact points to report any intimidation or approaches from older people potentially grooming them for criminal purposes, contact points should be well publicised and accessible.

Young people should be encouraged and supported through their schools and colleges to speak to Gang mentor's or access counselling if they have been directly affected. They should have access to a dedicated telephone line and online touch points. We know there is an embedded culture of apprehension to use existing services such as 'crime stoppers' so this is not effective, yet it forms part of the current advice.

Where a young person has been groomed or engaged in criminal activity by older gang members, the young person should, in the first instance, be offered counselling and support, family support should also be easily accessible. The emphasis should be placed on the child feeling protected and the opportunity should be taken to rebuild any broken family relationships, and to build trust between the child, the family and the authorities which, in turn, presents the opportunity to get important information that leads to arrests and keeps that child and other children safe.

Strategic, Intelligence led policing works

Strategic policing has been used effectively in the past, gang surveillance and the use of community policing, proved an effective way to engage with and serve the communities most at risk. The subsequent arrests were mostly effective and targeted the right people.

Stop and search is the most popular suggestion for tackling knife and violent crime, but this works best when carried out strategically, using an intelligence led approach and removing in-effective racial profiling that leads to the harassment of law-abiding citizens.

Change perceptions

One met officer recently spoke out and expressed his disappointment that people from wider communities were 'not outraged enough' by the epidemic of violent crime and murder on our streets. Whilst I agree with him wholeheartedly, and empathise with his frustrations, it is fair to suggest that part of the problem is that the issues are not being presented or approached in the same way as it would if it were predominantly affecting white communities.

Use the power of media

We need informational programs raising the issues and exploring the underlying problems. There are no media campaigns raising awareness for parents and the wider community to increase their understanding of the issues and intimidation methods being used to initiate young people into gangs.

There are not enough media campaigns highlighting the trauma faced by affected young people and their families, there are no posters on public transport, there are no adverts or infomercials on the TV offering advice to young people affected by gang crime, there are no national joint initiatives such as joint working between local organisations and organisations such as child line to offer support to younger children at risk of gang abuse and so on.

Why would the wider community perceive this as a societal issue when it is not being presented as such, but rather, it is presented as a Black issue that affects specific people in specific areas and is presented in the media as a fleeting news item!

Change the culture

To really be able to work on an effective strategy to tackle the issues affecting young people (particularly Black boys), we must change the culture that exists whereby, the issue is presented as only affecting Black or minority communities. The culture whereby young people and their families still feel that speaking out is 'grassing'.

The culture where these issues are separated, and wider society somehow miss the correlation between the people who are selling drugs and becoming embroiled in gangs, intimidation and violence, and the people taking drugs and putting themselves at risk of gangs, intimidation and violence. This is an issue that can potentially have a knock- on effect for any parent in the country.

Remove the glamour and highlight the abuse

When the issues are presented less glamorous, such as when we draw the comparisons between gang grooming and paedophile grooming, it changes everyone's perception of these perpetrators and greatly reduces the appeal of the gang leaders who are grooming young people.

When we present the mental and emotional abuse that children are suffering, it becomes a social issue that is everyone's problem.

When we put the harsh and ugly truth in front of people using mass media, it shows that this is a societal problem that is everyone's responsibility to tackle, it encourages people within the most affected communities to think and behave more strategically, it opens doors for building relationships between these communities and the police and authorities.

If these issues were affecting any other community on this level, we would have seen major prevention campaigns, adverts advising children about staying safe, information made available to affected families and so on. Why is this approach not being taken?

Improve the multidisciplinary approach

Everyone has a part to play in tackling these issues, but the first thing that needs to take place is a massive shift in culture, from the way the police and authorities are treating these children and their families, the way the issues are presented as news items that allow wider society to be comfortable in an 'othering process', the way mainstream radio such as BBC 1 Xtra are promoting music that incites violence, through to the way people in affected communities engage and report issues to the authorities.

This is of course, just one level of the issue. There are many more layers that need to be properly and publicly explored and addressed using a multi-disciplined approach that involves: Young people, parents, community representatives, psychologists, sociologists, drug and alcohol support, police, courts, social services (child protection), family support workers and the media.

Met Police are using 'racially discriminatory' Gangs Matrix database

The Metropolitan Police Service's 'Gangs Matrix' is the "wrong tool for the wrong problem" Amnesty International said, when it published its damning report into the gang-mapping database.

See extracts from the report.

8

The Gangs Matrix Report

The Metropolitan Police Service's gang-mapping database was launched in 2012 as part of a highly-politicised response to the 2011 London riots. It lists individuals as "gang nominals" with each given an automated violence ranking of green, amber or red. More than three-quarters (78%) of people on the Matrix are black, a disproportionate number given the Met's own figures show that only 27% of those responsible for serious youth violence are black. The youngest person on the Matrix in 2017 was 12 years old, and 99% of those listed are male.

The 55-page report 'Trapped in the Matrix', raises serious concerns about how individuals come to be placed on the database, how the information is shared with other agencies such as housing associations and schools, and the adverse effect being listed on the Matrix can have for the young black males who are disproportionately impacted. The researchers spoke to more than 30 professionals who use the Gangs Matrix, including the police and other organisations, as well as community members and young people affected by the Matrix.

Amnesty International UK's Director, said:

"There is clearly a huge problem with knife crime and youth violence in London, but the Gangs Matrix is not the answer. It's part of an unhelpful and racialised focus on the concept of gangs. Put simply, it's the wrong tool for the wrong problem...

The entire system is racially discriminatory, stigmatising young black men for the type of music they listen to or their social media behaviour, and perpetuating racial bias with potential impacts in all sorts of areas of their lives...Some police officers have been acting like they're in the wild west, making the false assumption that they can set up fake profiles and covertly befriend people online to monitor them without needing the appropriate search warrants. The Mayor of London needs to dismantle the Matrix unless he can bring it in line with international human rights standards."

The 'G' word': An unhelpful and racialised focus on the concept of the gang

The concept of 'the gang' and a gang member, or 'nominal', is vague and ill-defined, and based on racialised notions, the report finds.

Police officers raised concerns with Amnesty researchers about the conflation of gang crime with serious youth violence, even though in reality there is not as much overlap as presumed. The Mayor's Office for Policing and Crime found that more than 80% of all knife-crime incidents resulting in injury to a victim aged under 25 in London were deemed to be non-gang-related.

One Met Police officer told Amnesty:

"Gangs are, for the most part, a complete red herring… fixation with the term is unhelpful at every level."

The vagueness of the 'gang' label, and the large degree of discretion given to officers in assigning it, mean that the gang label is haphazardly used. In practice, it is disproportionately assigned to black men and boys, even where an individual's offending profile is otherwise the same as a white individual who is not so labelled.

This reflects a historic pattern of over-policing of Black, Asian and minority ethnic (BAME) communities.

Stafford Scott, from The Monitoring Group, a London-based campaigning organisation which challenges racism in policing,

argues that the Gangs Matrix is counterproductive and further erodes trust in and the legitimacy of the police. He said:

"Our community needs a police service to stop the murders, but the community won't engage with the police if they're forever coming up with oppressive forms. The Matrix reaffirms to the community that there is an institutionalised racist way of policing. It doesn't work, it just further marginalises this group of kids."

Gang Matrix explored

'Individuals who have never been involved with violent crime are routinely registered to the Gangs Matrix'. (Report from: Amnesty International)

Getting on the Matrix

The report uncovers a chaotic and inconsistent approach to how individuals come to be listed on the Matrix, which varies wildly from borough to borough in London.

The report warns that the threshold for getting added to the Matrix is very low, requiring just two pieces of "verifiable intelligence" with no clear guidance or criteria, while very wide discretion is given to both police and various other agencies. 'Partner agencies' - including housing associations, job centres and youth services at the borough level - can also put forward names to be added to the Gangs Matrix.

Individuals who have never been involved with violent crime are routinely registered to the Gangs Matrix. Even being a victim of a crime that the police link to a gang is viewed by the Metropolitan

Police as an indicator of a likelihood of

"subsequently becoming drawn in to involvement in

serious crime" and so can result in the individual

being placed on the Matrix.

9

Social media monitoring and racial profiling of

young black men

The report raises serious concerns about the practice of monitoring young people's behaviour online to determine possible gang affiliation.

The sharing of YouTube videos and other social media activity are used as potential criteria for adding names to the Matrix, with grime music videos featuring gang names or signs considered a particular possible indicator of likely gang affiliation. Amnesty's research raises concerns that people are therefore being profiled and monitored by police Gangs Units simply because of the subculture to which they belong and the people with whom they associate online.

Amnesty's research uncovered instances of police officers setting up fake social media profiles to monitor people they view as possible gang members.

That practice may in some instances be in breach of the Regulation of Investigatory Powers Act (RIPA). Amnesty's researchers were told that on at least one occasion, no RIPA warrant was obtained before undercover operations were carried out. One official even stated that they thought no such warrant was required because the profile created was linked to a council modem.

The report concludes that in the case of police officers "friending", or otherwise forming an online relationship with a potential person of interest, a covert human intelligence source authorisation (a warrant) is clearly required. Amnesty is calling for the Information Commissioner's Office (ICO) to urgently review the operation and the use of the Matrix by police and others.

Sharing the Matrix with other agencies

The report found that a range of non-police agencies have access to the Matrix, and so the stigma of suspicion or guilt related to inclusion on the Matrix can follow individuals through their interaction with a wide range of local services, including job centres, housing associations and schools.

Data sharing may lead to negative outcomes in other areas of individual's lives, such as in their access to housing, with both a former housing officer and a member of staff at a Borough Gangs Unit describing the issuing of eviction notices as a routine tactic used to put pressure on a 'nominal'.

This not only affects those on the Matrix but, in the case of housing, also their siblings and other family members. Again, these negative impacts disproportionately affect young black boys and men. Amnesty is particularly concerned that the broad sharing of the Matrix with partner agencies raises a number of conflicts with the Data Protection Act and accompanying Code of Conduct and guidance.

10

Trapped on the Matrix

Officials reported a general pressure from the police in the Gangs Units to "keep people on" the Matrix in case they later went on to commit a violent offence. The report found the processes surrounding review of inclusion on the Matrix inadequate given the sensitivity of the data held, including on children as young as 12.

Amnesty called for the ICO to urgently open a full public investigation into the Matrix and its use, including whether it complies with data protection laws. Amnesty also called for Mayor of London Sadiq Khan to respond to the concerns raised in the report, with a view to scrapping the Matrix if it cannot be brought in line with international human rights standards.

(Source: Amnesty International's report on the Gang Matrix).

The issues surrounding violent crime, knife crime, so called gang activity and the impact on young people, families and communities across the country, will not be tackled using the current methods which have all proven to be ineffective and utterly useless. They do nothing more than create a cycle of frustration, repeat offending, mistrust and disengagement.

Furthermore, an outdated approach whereby organisations fight and compete over small scraps of funding to create services that become as territorial as the so-called gangs they work with - must change! This approach at a grass roots level only perpetuates territorial rivalry. The culture of working in this way is so embedded it will need a strategic approach to change it for the better.

Young people should be encouraged to use centralised services, they should be encouraged to mix from a young age, activities and services should be neutral and bring young people together and be instrumental in reversing the 'othering' process that is currently allowed to develop and fuel rivalry.

The 'To do list' is long. But new strategic approaches are necessary because political rhetoric and endless discussion is not preventing the deaths of young people on Britain's streets. Creating opportunities to blame teachers and A&E staff with the newly suggested public responsibility approach, appears at first glance to be another useless strategy that will have no impact at all.

Knife crime has become big business for too many, from funded groups to prison contractors such as G4S to the funeral industry. It's time we put the protection and safety of children at the heart of any strategy and create economic and social resources to ensure they reap the benefits of living in one of the richest countries in the world.

Printed in Great Britain
by Amazon

38446600R00035